A Pocket Guide to Converse
Jessica Bumpus

A Pocket Guide
to Converse

Jessica Bumpus

Laurence King

Contents

I was in my mid-teens when I bought my first Converse sneakers, a pair of classic high-top All Stars in pink. They had been purchased on a trip down to London one summer and I had been very excited to get them – a significant and serious addition to my footwear collection at the time, akin to a 'designer' shoe. I wore them on my first day at university. Through love and wear – with everything from jeans to party dresses – they eventually turned nearly white. When I worked as an intern at a cool magazine, I also acquired a cream pair of All Stars that had been customized by a stylist for a shoot, and these became a prized possession.

But this isn't a story about me. This is the story of an iconic brand whose reach has been far and wide over the century and more that it has been in existence. Starting from humble beginnings as a rubber shoe manufacturer in Massachusetts, US, in 1908, helmed by one Marquis Mills Converse, the company would go on to make a name for itself in the world of basketball circa 1922 – care of its star salesman, Chuck Taylor, after whom its most famous shoes were named.

After breaking into the lifestyle arena as the favoured footwear of skaters and punks, Converse became as much a badge of underground cool as a legend of American sportswear. At the first ever Olympic basketball championships, held in 1936 in Berlin, the Americans wore All Stars with red and blue stripes; fast-forward 50 years, and the same sneaker style was worn by Matthew Broderick in the beloved teen comedy *Ferris Bueller's Day Off*. There are plenty more instances where Converse has made both cult and commercial film cameos, and we'll reveal more about those later.

There are perhaps few brands whose name can act as the missing link between *The Simpsons*, grunge icon Kurt Cobain and the elegant French fashion designer Isabel Marant as Converse can – and a great many more could be added to this eclectic list. The brand has made each the subject of a fruitful collaboration, ensuring the continued relevancy of its now legendary colourful canvas sneakers. They may have had their start in the sporting arena, but they have now become a firm favourite among fashion insiders, and not only to be worn – *Vogue* editors have revealed that they stash pairs away in their kit for shoots, so essential are they for bringing a certain vibe.

Converse's All Star logo is now as iconic as Christian Louboutin's red sole, the label on Levi's jeans and the interlocking G buckle of a Gucci belt. The sneakers have appeared on the feet of stars including Rihanna, Avril Lavigne and Timothée Chalamet, and have been famously worn on the red carpet by Kristen Stewart, which back in the noughties was deemed a very daring thing to do. In 2012, when she wore them again at an awards ceremony, *British Vogue* reported that the actress said she was able to get around and sign more autographs for fans in the flats. In advertising campaigns throughout the years, comfort and ease have been a key part of the brand's messaging.

Beyond their rich and engaging history both on and off the court, what stands out about a pair of Converse is their design. They are instantly recognizable, especially with their palette of bright shades (including, amongst others, Sunflower, Watermelon Slushy, Pink Foam, Viper Violet and Amazon Green). Arguably, it is a simpler design than most sneaker brands, having never fundamentally changed too much – though there have been new additions, design tweaks and styles introduced along the way.

Much of the appeal of Converse sneakers lies in the sense of retro-nostalgia they provoke, with a feel that is quintessentially American. Often made from canvas, they are indeed a blank canvas for the wearer's own personal style, which is the kind of thinking the brand encourages, their website declaring, 'When you wear Converse products, you create a culture of authentic street style simply by being yourself.'

Today, Converse is owned by Nike, Inc., having been bought in 2003 for a reported sum of over US$300 million. Iconic styles from the 1980s have been revived and the brand has extended into apparel, continuing to be a high-street staple. Of course, none of this would have been possible had it not been for that rubber shoe factory back in 1908.

History

There are two names to note when it comes to the history of Converse: Marquis Mills Converse, the company's namesake, and Charles Hollis Taylor, or Chuck Taylor, arguably the original face of the brand. While it was the former who founded the Converse Rubber Shoe Company in Malden, Massachusetts, in the early 20th century, it is the latter who is now regarded as having been pivotal in the marketing of the brand.

Marquis Mills Converse preceded Chuck Taylor, and there is perhaps less known about him than there is about Taylor. Yet without Converse, there would have been no shoe company at all. Converse, the company, had originally been conceived in 1890. Marquis Mills was a manager at a footwear manufacturer at the time, and he established Converse & Pike along with a business partner. It was originally a wholesale operation, selling rubber boots to Boston retailers.

RIGHT: Chuck Taylor, salesman and promoter of the Converse All Star.

As luck, or fate, would have it, basketball came bounding into the arena a year later and an inextricable link between Converse and the sport would soon be formed. Despite becoming prominent in various other sports and cultural scenes since then, basketball has remained core to the brand to this day, with even the skate shoes having come directly from the court.

Basketball's invention is attributed to James Naismith, a physical education teacher, in 1891. Serendipitously, its invention also took place in Massachusetts – in Springfield, less than 160 km (100 miles) from the Converse headquarters. The Canadian–American teacher apparently conceived basketball as a way to make physical education less dangerous and more enjoyable. The new game took on elements of field hockey, American football and soccer, and would become a particular favourite with colleges. Part of its appeal was that it required less space than the games it had borrowed from. It quickly became popular with young people and a professional league was formed in 1898. All of this would prove significant in the story of Converse, which as yet hadn't found its basketball feet.

LEFT: Basketball player Oscar Robertson wearing Converse in 1958. Basketball and Converse would become synonymous.

Around the turn of the century, Converse's partner, Pike, departed and the company changed its name to M.M. Converse, but both family problems and instability in the rubber market forced the sale of the business. Undeterred, by 1908 Converse had started up the Converse Rubber Shoe Company with US$250,000 of venture capital (estimates put that sum at around US$6.5 million today).

The company aimed to produce a range of rubber products, including car tyres, galoshes (a type of rubber overshoe) and tennis shoes – which are thought to have morphed into the basketball line. (Later on Converse would also promote tennis shoes, and in an advert from 1977, the former US world number one Chris Evert is shown wearing the Converse model bearing her name on the court). The first Converse factory was up and running before the end of the decade, and its first Converse shoe emerged in 1909.

The Birth of Sneakers

The term 'sneakers' is thought to have come into use during the 1880s in the US. Apparently, it referred to the quiet rubber soles of the shoes, which meant you could 'sneak up' on people. Whether true or not, it makes for a fun piece of trivia. There was a good deal of activity in the rubber shoe market during the 19th and early 20th centuries. In 1839, the American inventor Charles Goodyear created vulcanized rubber, which made it possible to use the material commercially, and this is what would be used for sneakers. The very first sneakers, though, are thought to have been the 'sand shoes' made by the Liverpool Rubber Company in the UK. These were canvas with rubber soles and, as the name suggests, were often worn at the beach. These were later renamed plimsolls.

The first Converse shoe emerged in 1909.

Recreational sports, such as croquet, had started to become popular towards the end of the 19th century, and as a result there was a growing demand for the right kind of footwear. The US Rubber Company began selling modified versions of the plimsoll – the sneaker – in 1892, which had laces and thicker rubber soles, and then introduced Keds in 1916, which proved especially popular with women. Meanwhile, the early seeds were sown for the Puma and Adidas brands in 1924, when Adolf Dassler and his brother Rudolf set up the Dassler Brothers Shoe Factory in Germany. In 1948, rivalry between the pair caused them to split the company in two, with Rudolf creating Ruda – later Puma – and Adolf setting up Adidas. All of this would play a part in the evolution of the Converse brand.

By 1910, Converse claimed it was making 5,500 pairs of galoshes a day, and by the middle of the decade

ABOVE: Advert for the Non-Skid from 1920.

it had expanded into athletics shoes, introducing a shoe called the Non-Skid. This had been specifically designed for basketball: a canvas style featuring a small capped toe and a distinctive diamond tread pattern, which enabled ease of movement in different directions and the ability to stop quickly – ideal on the basketball court. The Non-Skid was reissued as the All Star in 1919 and is, according to Converse, the 'great-grandfather of today's Chuck'. The shoe received a name tweak again in the early 1930s, when it became the Chuck Taylor All Star – now commonly referred to as 'Chucks'.

World's First Sports Promoter

Chuck Taylor, the man, had joined Converse in
the early 1920s after applying for a sales job. It
turned out to be a fortuitous move, and he would
become a pioneer of sports marketing. Taylor was
an early brand ambassador, perhaps akin to the
mega sports stars of today, important enough that
his name was included on the sneaker's ankle patch
logo in 1934. Inside the eye-catching circular patch,
on either side of the iconic star, the words 'Chuck'
and 'Taylor' were added. It is still there today
on the classic All Star design, the style he
made famous and with which he has
become most associated – quite the
lasting legacy for the salesman.
According to the *New York Times*'
sports magazine *The Athletic*,
1934 was also the year that
Converse struck its first licensing
deal with Disney, putting Mickey
Mouse on the shoe.

ABOVE: Chuck
Taylor's name
on the All Star
ankle patch.

Chuck Taylor is so synonymous with
Converse that one could easily be forgiven for
thinking he had founded the company in the first
place. Similarly, one could assume – and it has been
suggested numerous times – that Taylor had a
helping hand in designing the legendary shoe that
bears his name. This footwear myth has, however,
been debunked. In an interview with the online
menswear platform Mr Porter in 2020, Elizabeth

Semmelhack, the creative director and senior curator of the Bata Shoe Museum in Toronto, and a prolific author of books on sneaker history and culture, insisted that 'there's actually no proof of that' – something that's backed up by Converse's own records.

Sam Smallidge, the brand's in-house archivist, has suggested that Taylor might have received feedback from basketball coaches and passed that along, but the idea that he was in the workshop was not realistic: 'He was more of a coaches' coach and a salesman than anything else.' Along the way, though, sneaker history has had a habit of rewriting and embellishing upon this.

Should you have thought Chuck Taylor was perhaps not even real, you could also be forgiven – as sneaker heroes go, there has not been so much written about him. What little we do know, according to the Naismith Memorial Basketball Hall of Fame, is that he was born in Brown County, Indiana, in 1901, and was a two-time All-State selection on Columbus High School's basketball team, and a journeyman jump shooter who went on to play for 11 professional seasons.

He was more of a coaches' coach and a salesman than anything else.

During the early years of basketball, various shoe and rubber companies started their own basketball teams, which would tour the country to advertise their products; the basketball teams and matches became a kind of promotional tool. Chuck Taylor headed up the Converse team, which was known as the All Stars – of course! A key sales strategy he employed was to put on 'clinics' for the team coaches, then take them to sports stores to order Converse shoes; the idea was that the coaches would remember who taught them to play basketball (Chuck Taylor), who he worked for (Converse), and which shoes he was selling (All Stars).

Interestingly, it is not even known if Taylor was any good on the court (though, again, some accounts pitch him as being a basketball star *as well* as the Converse design mastermind). His major talent appears to have been his ability to generate interest in basketball, which made the game well known, and consequently Converse, too.

Converse claimed to be the number one shoe in America by 1955, accounting for 80 per cent of the sneaker footwear market.

Business was said to be booming, but in 1929 Converse faced bankruptcy as a result of debts incurred from failed attempts to make car tyres. The Great Depression also began that year. But the decade wasn't all bad for the brand. It had come up with a plan to boost its sales, capitalizing on their star salesman's success by adding his name to the All Stars' ankle patch. Few others through history can boast such an accolade – most famously Stan Smith (and the Adidas tennis shoe he inspired) and Michael Jordan (and Nike's Air Jordan) – but there are not many, and certainly not back then.

By this point, the Converse brand had become synonymous with basketball, which would feature as an Olympic event for the first time at the 1936 Berlin games. The Americans wore their red-and-blue striped All Stars and won gold. And in 1939, the first National Collegiate Athletics Association (NCAA) championship took place, with both teams sporting Converse. The brand and the world it had helped to create was beginning to take shape.

When America entered World War Two in 1941, Converse pivoted its production to kitting out American troops with rubberized footwear, protective suits and coats (only a small number of All Stars were available to the public at this time). Taylor himself reportedly served as a captain in the US Air Force and coached regional basketball teams. Because GIs did their fitness training in Converse high tops, it has been said that they became the unofficial training shoe of the US Armed Forces.

Production of athletics footwear began again after the war ended. The National Basketball League (NBL) and the Basketball Association of America (BAA) merged in 1949 to create the National Basketball Association (NBA), and on most players' feet, reportedly, was a pair of Converse sneakers. Converse claimed to be the number one shoe in America by 1955, accounting for 80 per cent of the sneaker footwear market.

With 1957 came a new development – the low-top All Stars. This 'Oxford' iteration was a result of feedback from players and coaches who wanted a less restrictive version of the All Stars, something that allowed more ankle mobility. Cut to fit below the ankle, these were perhaps always a little more casual and more suitable for off-court use – a low-key take on the boating shoe, and the sort of easy shoe that chimed with the lifestyle direction the brand would start to move towards in later years.

The low-top brought Converse to the attention of a new audience, surfers among them, who found they could easily kick them off and enjoyed their comfort and feel. The brand credits the 1960s as the era in which it experienced its 'rebirth as a lifestyle shoe'.

Chuck Taylor was inducted into the Naismith Memorial Basketball Hall of Fame in 1969 – the facility is named after the man who invented the game and located in Springfield, Massachusetts, the birthplace of the sport. That same year, as he neared his 68th birthday, Taylor reportedly died of a heart attack. In so many ways, it was the end of an era.

LEFT: Elvis Presley wearing Converse in *Follow That Dream* (1962).

Style Notes

A key moment in Converse history came in 1971. Besides Chuck Taylor and the star insignia, one of the things the brand is best known for is its rainbow colour palette, which makes the shoes so unique and recognizable. It was in this year that Converse

BELOW: The ability to customize their sneakers has always been key to Converse's appeal.

debuted coloured canvas, said to be a way for collegiate teams to match their school colours and for those watching to show their support.

As the brand evolved, Converse became closely associated with the counterculture, which stressed the importance of individuality. Customization remains key for both the Converse design repertoire and for its audience, and part of the shoes' genius is that, for the most part, they are a literal blank canvas. Head to the website these days and 'Start With a Blank' to create your own design, from colour and print to lining. Self-expression has become an important part of the brand's DNA, and today campaigns are built around this notion. Converse By You x Billie Eilish, to give a recent example, is at once about community and creativity as well as individualism and freedom – all of which are inherent brand traits.

Part of the shoes' genius is that, for the most part, they are a literal blank canvas.

In addition, well-worn Converse shoes are seen as a badge of honour in the sneaker world. By the 1970s, Converse had infiltrated the punk scene, worn by edgy proto-punk rockers the Ramones, among others. They were then adopted by heavy metal

fans in the 1980s, and the influential grunge scene in the 1990s – of which they were an integral part, loved for their bashed-up aesthetic, which chimed with that tribe's lo-fi vibe. All of these settings appeared radically different from the pristine all-American team spirit of the sport that had first inspired them. Yet the one thing they all had in common was their community focus, added to the fact that the shoes have always managed to transcend style tribes.

It was in the 1980s that Converse also started to make notable appearances on screen (though they

LEFT: The Ramones in 1978.

ABOVE: Matthew Broderick in *Ferris Bueller's Day Off* (1986).

had appeared in films and TV since the 1950s), with cameos in *Back to the Future* and *Ferris Bueller's Day Off*, broadening the reach of the sneaker, which now started to tread towards cult style status.

A Changing Field

While Converse might have gained a new following in the 1970s, its popularity began to dwindle on court, thanks to fellow sneaker competitors, and the company ran into business difficulties. That said, the mid-1970s saw the introduction of the star chevron insignia, which featured on various designs in place of the circle ankle patch, including the new Pro Leather design. Originally released in 1976, the Pro Leather was famously worn by the NBA's Julius Erving, a.k.a. 'Dr. J' – one of the game's star players and a court legend. Converse claims the Pro Leather was worn by more college and professional players than any other shoe in history.

It was during the 1980s that the brand experienced what it describes as its 'performance era'. Having established a biomechanics lab to research and develop products that would improve performance and comfort, it created high-tech midsole cushioning systems and introduced the Fastbreak basketball shoe. This lightweight and breathable

LEFT: Michael Jordan wearing Converse Fastbreak for the 1984 Olympic trials.

shoe debuted in 1983 and became front and centre on the court, worn by Michael Jordan during the 1984 Olympic trials. It has since been re-engineered for skateboarding and updated to combine archival flourishes with design durability.

The keep-fit craze of the 1980s also saw a surge of interest in jogging, and Converse was not immune, developing biomechanical running shoes. Furthermore, Converse became the official footwear sponsor of the 1984 Summer Olympics, held in LA. In fact, as the brand proudly states, its shoes appeared in final medal rounds at every Olympic competition between 1936 and 1988. Pretty impressive.

The Chuck Taylor All Star, however, was last worn in the NBA in 1986, and the brand was out of the game completely by the early 2010s. Kelly Oubre Jr., the US pro basketball player for the Philadelphia 76ers, is credited with helping the brand get back into the basketball conversation when he signed on their campaign roster and helped to revamp the All Star Pro BB in 2019 (see page 59). In the 2020s, Shai Gilgeous-Alexander, has also contributed to this revival (see pages 66–68).

Looking Forward

By the 1990s, Converse had well and truly scooted beyond the boards of the basketball court and into the realms of pop culture and daily life. A pair of Converse Stars & Bars, a design defined by its

ABOVE: Converse was the official footwear
sponsor of the 1984 Olympics.

midfoot decoration of said stars and bars, was donated to the Smithsonian in 1992, and by the end of the decade, 550 million pairs of Chuck Taylor All Stars had been produced.

But the brand's road hasn't always been an easy one. Over the course of its over a century-long history, Converse has had a series of owners, beginning when financial troubles hit in 1929 and the president of Hodgman Rubber Company, Mitchell B. Kaufman, took over from Marquis Mills Converse. So the story goes, the company was sold just a year later to Albert Welchester, who remained in charge until the 1930s, when he could no longer afford the business. Converse was then sold to the Stone family, who owned it until 1972, when it was acquired by Eltra Corporation, which later handed control of it over to their parent company, Allied Corporation, in the late 1970s. Eltra Corporation is thought to have bought it back in the early 1980s. Interco Inc. acquired Converse in 1986, but went bankrupt in 1991. In the early 2000s, Converse lost its exclusive relationship with the NBA, and following what it has called some 'short-sighted decisions', entered into bankruptcy in 2001.

And then along came Nike, in 2003, which meant Converse's impact would be felt once more. Following a time of rebirth, the *New York Times* reported in 2014 that Converse had accused 31 companies of trademark infringement, and 22 separate lawsuits had been filed in a bid to protect its Chuck Taylor All Stars.

Over the past 20 years, apparel has been added to the Converse range, and the brand often engages in collaborations with high-profile names, having expanded its influence in the fashion sphere (not least because fashion designers and off-duty models wear the sneakers). It has debuted more collaborations than is possible to keep up with, and it has become the shoe of choice for a new generation of emo and alt-pop stars as well as celebrities, from indie to mainstream.

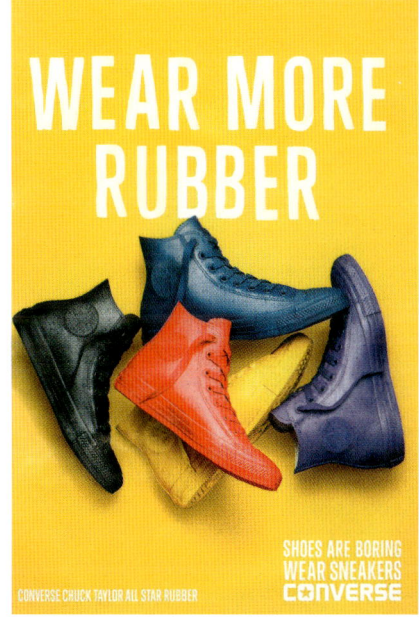

WEAR MORE RUBBER

CONVERSE CHUCK TAYLOR ALL STAR RUBBER

SHOES ARE BORING
WEAR SNEAKERS
CONVERSE

Today, Jared Carver is the president and chief executive officer of the Nike-owned brand and he is tasked with continuing the legacy started by Taylor and Marquis Mills Converse over a century ago. He was appointed to the role in 2023. That same year, the sneaker industry was estimated to generate more than US$75 billion in sales worldwide. With a heritage spanning the decades, and styles that have kept pace with the times as well as maintaining its legendary original designs, Converse will no doubt have contributed to a significant portion of that.

ABOVE: From its origins as a rubber shoe company to today, Converse has remained stylish and relevant. Advert from 2010s.

High tops, low tops, platforms, boots, slip-ons – all available in a dizzying array of colours and patterns as well as being uniquely customizable . . . there are plenty of decisions to be made today when it comes to buying a pair of Converse. The styles and designs have evolved and expanded to appeal to a world far beyond the confines of the court, but that is where the most famous Converse designs began.

All Star

The Converse All Star is easily recognized, with its rubber outsoles bearing the diamond tread pattern, its distinctive toecap, canvas upper, eyelets for laces and ventilation, and the ankle patch on the inside of each shoe. On the back of the heel, it bears the legend 'All Star'. The shoe still comes in classic black and white, as well as any number of other hues and patterns. It is a slim sneaker, and it is unisex (though the Converse website does split its offerings into men's and women's styles).

RIGHT: Alex Winter and Keanu Reeves wearing Converse All Stars in *Bill and Ted's Excellent Adventure* (1989).

There is only one All Star.®
Only Converse makes it.
Only sporting goods dealers sell it.

The Converse All Star is basketball's shoe. This year 8 out of 10 players in every major college and junior college tournament wore Converse All Stars. Converse All Stars have been worn by every U.S. Olympic Team since 1936, and All Stars have been selected again by the U.S. Olympic Committee for the 1976 Olympics. They are available in 10 team colors, 5 action styles in suede, leather and canvas.

★ **converse**

an **Eltra** company

This is the shoe that started everything, beginning life as the Non-Skid and becoming the All Star, a favourite of the US Armed Forces. After World War Two, the solid black design changed to a black and white look, with white laces, toe caps and outer wraps, and by 1948 the All Stars took on the appearance we recognize in the core models of today.

The 1940s, 1950s and 1960s are now seen as the glory days of the Chuck Taylor All Star. It makes sense, as that early Americana feel was very much entrenched during those decades, during which Converse was also still a key player on the basketball scene. The 1970s were a time of significant change in the sport, and by the 1980s, rivals such as Nike (which now owns Converse) and Reebok came into the picture.

In earlier years, simply referring to your 'Cons' was enough for everyone to know you were talking about your Chuck Taylor All Stars. But following the introduction of so many new styles, 'Chucks' emerged as the new informal term for them. Today, 'Cons' more specifically refers to the brand's skateboarding series, and there are clear distinctions between models and their use – the terminology around Converse sneakers is extensive.

LEFT: Advert for the Converse All Star from the 1970s.

It's been noted that the Converse All Star wasn't the first basketball sneaker in history, and nor was it the brand's first venture into the sports shoe market (it produced tennis shoes before it produced basketball sneakers), but it remains its best-known design, more or less untouched since its inception.

That is, until 2015, when along came the Converse Chuck II, the first redesign since the 1930s. In 2015, Geoff Cottrill, then chief marketing officer at Converse, told British lifestyle magazine Dazed Digital, 'We redesigned everything, yet redesigned nothing.' He elaborated, 'We focused on the comfort that customers were asking us for.' This resulted in a design that was strikingly similar to the original (as one would expect), but with tweaks to the details: a Nike sockliner, for example, as well as a foam-padded collar and a padded tongue. According to the *New York Times*, the style underwent 16

alterations in total in a bid to improve the comfort. But by 2017 they had ceased production – so if you're lucky enough to own a pair, that surely makes them all the more collectible.

Chuck 70

More successful than the All Star rebrand, however, was the Chuck 70, introduced in 2013. This was a modern reinterpretation of the classic Chuck Taylor All Star – so similar in looks, in fact, that even Converse itself notes that unless you are a 'sneaker connoisseur, it's difficult to find the differences'.

BELOW: Red suede Chuck 70s.

ABOVE: The Chuck 70 has been the basis for a series of collaborations between Missoni and Converse.

But differences do exist, upon close inspection. The focus here is on durability and stability: there is a thicker midsole, there for increased shock absorption; the rubber toe has a bumper effect; and there is reinforced stitching around the toecap as well as double-ply canvas on the upper for structural support, making it more hardwearing. It does feature the retro Converse patch on the ankle as well – it's worth noting that, as styles and designs have developed, not all Converse sneakers have this.

A vintage off-white varnish is used on the sole rather than them being pristine white – an ode to the original look of the 1970s Chuck Taylor All Stars.

Further nods to the original come by way of old-school detailing, which has been faithfully recreated: the nickel-plated eyelets and nylon webbing heel strip, for example. The idea is that the shoe retains the retro feel but with modern comfort in mind.

The Chuck 70 has provided the basis for a series of collaborations with various artists and designers over the years, including high-fashion brands Maison Margiela and Missoni, and – more within its own wheelhouse – Off-White and Carhartt.

The wunderkind designer Jonathan Anderson (of JW Anderson, and also Loewe) has imagined and reimagined the Chuck 70 on various occasions over the years (see pages 127–129). Known for its chunkier profile compared to the Chuck Taylor, a more extreme version of the Chuck 70 could be considered the Run Star Hike, on which the brand had also partnered with Anderson originally. Boasting a jagged platform – a nod to a hiking boot – it's a bold design, or, as Converse has described it, 'loud'.

Along with the All Star, the Chuck 70 has achieved screen-icon status, having made appearances in numerous movies and TV shows. The appeal of Converse is that the design doesn't belong solely to the sports shoe category. They are shoes for real life – running errands, enjoying a weekend, for anyone and everyone, anywhere. And the more contemporary Converse campaigns speak to an authenticity that resonates with its fanbase.

According to Hal Peterson, superfan and author of *Chucks! The Phenomenon of Converse*, one of the reasons for the sneakers' popularity has been their rubber-and-canvas design, which appeals to vegetarians (although Chucks, and other styles, do come in leather as well). Peterson's book was first published in 2007, but in today's sustainably minded world, he – and Converse – were ahead of the game. In recent years, sustainability is something the brand has explored further with upcycled versions of their shoes.

The Upcycled Flannel Chuck 70 incorporates uppers made from post-consumer flannel. An upcycled capsule collection was first launched in 2015 as an in-house experiment, and in 2017 Converse teamed up with textile-sourcing partner and recycler Beyond Retro so that the product could be scaled up for consumers to buy.

Brandon Avery, vice president of global innovation at Converse, summarized the development process for *Glossy Magazine* in 2023, saying: 'The initial in-house experiment served as the foundation for an important question: What can't you make the Chuck Taylor [style] out of? Our team found that the only limit is imagination. We can make our footwear out of just about anything: automobile seats, coats and even waterproof envelopes.' Converse, Avery explained, had visited a factory in India to work through the upcycling process. No new flannel was produced and, on average, two pairs of Converse Upcycled Flannel Chuck 70s uppers were crafted per pre-loved flannel shirt.

Further upcycled capsules debuted in 2019 and 2022, featuring denim and velvet. In addition, Converse has been working to make the rubber in its shoes more sustainable, with the goal of achieving 10 per cent recycled rubber content. There is also something very sustainable about the fact that Converse fans like to wear their shoes until they fall apart.

One Star

In 1974, Converse debuted a low-top suede version of the Chuck Taylor, this time with one star on the

BELOW: Alexis Sablone x One Star Pro Low.

outside of the sneaker. The One Star was a close replica of the Suede Leather All Star that had come before it. The design, and its spinoffs, became a hit when they were reissued in the 1990s, and this time around they became especially popular among skateboarders.

The One Star Pro features upgraded cushioning and rubber-backed suede for maximum durability, while elastic gussets mean the tongue is locked in. In addition to Jack Purcell's and All Stars, Nirvana's Kurt Cobain often wore One Stars following their revival in the 1990s, and today they have been spotted on the feet of actress Millie Bobby Brown and US rapper Tyler, The Creator – who have both collaborated on sneaker designs.

Some consider the One Star Pro an unsung hero within the Converse stable. Aesthetically, these shoes have a retro 1970s feel (the 1970s and the 1990s have a style synergy owing to fashion's 20-year cycle) and, because of their skateboarding slant, are chunkier and more durable, typically coming in leather and suede as opposed to canvas.

LEFT: Tyler, The Creator wearing One Stars.

Jack Purcell

Another 'low-key legend', as described by Converse, is the Jack Purcell, which was named after the Canadian-born world badminton champion of that name. It is a low-top refined style of shoe with layers of cushioning for comfort and a durable canvas upper to give the classic Converse feel.

During the 1930s, Purcell partnered with the B.F. Goodrich Company, a rubber tyre manufacturing business, to create on-court shoes that would help him with his positioning and offer additional support. The result, in 1935, was a pair of sneakers with a signature 'smile' on the vulcanized toepiece. They featured a moulded non-skid outsole, an extra-thick spongey sole, and a wedge in the heel that reduced strain on the leg muscles.

ABOVE: Advert for Jack Purcells from the 1970s.

A pair of sneakers with a signature 'smile' on the vulcanized toepiece.

LEFT: Kurt Cobain wearing Jack Purcells (right) with Courtney Love (left) at the 1993 MTV Video Music Awards.

These shoes were successful off the court, too, their minimal branding making them a versatile item. By the 1950s the shoes had become the off-duty footwear of choice for both James Dean (whose image features in a 1989 advert, looking effortlessly debonair) and the ever-stylish actor Steve McQueen. Elvis Presley and George Harrison also wore Jack Purcells. During the 1970s, Converse acquired the rights to the shoe and the brand has evolved it with various tweaks over the years.

Kurt Cobain wore Jack Purcell's in the nineties. The actress Selena Gomez is reportedly a fan of the sneakers, and in 2019 the US rapper A$AP Nast collaborated with Converse on his own range of Jack Purcells (he had already collaborated with Converse on the Chuck Taylor All Star 70 in 2017). These came in a mid-top silhouette and featured flame detailing on the outer. Sneaker fan sites s uch as Sneaker Freaker have called for there to be a modern collaboration between BFGoodrich and Converse to bring back some of the original branding for the 90th anniversary of the Jack Purcell.

Converse Weapon

In the 1980s, along came the Converse Weapon, which was accompanied by some pretty iconic advertising featuring two of basketball's all-time

RIGHT: Party to celebrate the 75th anniversary of the Jack Purcell in 2010.

legends, Magic Johnson and Larry Bird. They were also fierce rivals who played for opposing teams, the LA Lakers and the Boston Celtics (see pages 64–66), which made the naming of the shoe a little loaded.

It has often been pointed out that before Michael Jordan's Air Jordans became the NBA's footwear of choice, it was the Converse Weapon that stole the show. Released in 1986, the shoes were famously worn by both Bird and Johnson, but they were also worn by pretty much all the NBA stars in the late 1980s (except Jordan, though he had worn a pair of Converse Fastbreaks in the 1984 Olympic trials; see page 29).

The design was a bulky high top, and considered the brand's most advanced shoe at the time. It built on the Chuck Taylor legacy and continued in the vein of Julius Erving's Pro Leather model (see page 29). The upper was leather and featured padding in the ankle and heel for added comfort. It was a move on from those early All Stars, which mostly relied on the ankle patch for support and padding. The Weapon was well noted for its vibrant colour palette. A low-top version was also produced.

The Weapon's popularity waned, however, as Nike's Air Jordan – with a little help from Michael Jordan

LEFT: Larry Bird wearing Converse Weapons on the basketball court in 1991.

– took off and became *the* shoe of basketball. Many of the players who had worn the Converse Weapon also began to fade from the limelight. Four decades later though, in 2021, Converse relaunched the Weapon as part of its CX line. For this series, Converse added a midsole made of CX foam for impact absorption and 'game-changing comfort'.

The relaunch also involved a series of collaborations, further expanding Converse's reach, including with Rick Owens and his DRKSHDW label (see pages 135–37). The American fashion designer regularly shows his wares during Paris Fashion Week, and they are known for their sense of otherworldliness, dystopian beauty and jarring aesthetic. Owens approached his redesign of the Weapon, called TURBOWPN, in the same spirit, making it even chunkier and with an extended tongue. The ability of the Converse Weapon to tap into nostalgia as well as new technology is making it relevant once more.

Run Star

Chunkier Converse models include those in the Run Star series, such as the Run Star Hike, introduced in 2019, the Run Star Motion, released in 2021, and 2022's Run Star Legacy. They all take the Chuck Taylor style to lofty new heights, and sometimes angles, with platform and wedge designs.

RIGHT: Model wearing Rick Owens x Converse TURBOWPN design.

The Run Star Hike (see pages 127–28) is striking for its two-tone sawtooth-style rubber outsole for increased grip; it also has a rounded heel that feels rather futuristic and, in conjunction with the moulded platform sole, gives it a solid and sturdy appearance. It features the All Star ankle patch and the classic Chuck Taylor All Star canvas with rubber toecap (but is also available in leather), as well as a SmartFoam sockliner for extra cushioning. It displays one star on the heel.

The design was introduced as a result of the penchant for chunky sneakers in the 1990s and early 2000s (think of the Spice Girls' platform sneaker moment), and because it lent itself to comfort. Converse said: 'The goal was to create a more rugged look for the classic Chuck Taylor All Star. By incorporating the two-tone sawtooth tread from the original Converse Run Star sneaker on a platform sole, the Run Star Hike was born.' The Legacy version features a distorted heel, while the Motion is the chunkiest of them all.

In June 2024, Converse introduced the Run Star Trainer, which of them all looks most like a standard sneaker, albeit one 'combining retro and modern aesthetics drawn from nearly 20 of the brand's heritage classics', according to the press release.

LEFT: The Run Star Motion.

ABOVE: The Run
Star Trainer.

'The silhouette is inspired by Converse's deep history in sport but designed for modern life – enabling new styling for those who value versatility, self-expression and comfort.' It comes in five bold colourways and has a low-cut profile, making it suitable for many different sports. It has joined a series of new introductions from Converse, which include the De Luxe Wedge, Heeled and Squared offerings. This all feels quite fashion and more in line with some of the collaborations, but notably, as the brand itself said, it chimed with their consumers wanting more opportunities for self-expression.

Knee High

It is the Converse community that is in part responsible for the return of the Knee High, an early noughties classic, which was also

RIGHT: Halsey performing in Knee Highs at the 2024 MTV Video Music Awards.

reintroduced in June 2024. Having been first released in 2006, they were discontinued in the 2010s and had become a topic of conversation on TikTok. The noughties have recently enjoyed a mass resurgence of influence in fashion. This, coupled with the popularity and growth of resale sites, meant it was the Knee High's turn. The all-the-way-to-the-knee version of the Chuck Taylor started to appear on Depop and eBay, with prices as high as $350. Fans from all over the world apparently asked for the statement shoe to be reissued. In 2023, in a highly effective publicity stunt, Converse posted a video highlighting the swarm of comments that begged for the shoes' return on TikTok. Then, a year later, the Chuck Taylor All Star XXHi was back!

The Knee High, an early noughties classic, was reintroduced in June 2024.

The shoe retains the original design DNA and features a 14-inch canvas upper, which hugs the calf and stops below the knee. A full-length zipper runs down the back so that they are easy to put on, and they also come with extra-long laces.

First launching in the classic black and white colourways, the black sold out instantly. The design may have been unconventional, but it drew a crowd among those who wanted something different.

All Star Also-rans

Along with super high, super low, and everything in between, there are also fold-over or roll-down All Stars. It might be surprising to learn that Converse has also produced mules, or clogs, slip-on styles that riff on its One Star designs and the Chuck 70 in recycled canvas, as well as techy sandals. There have also been loafers with a thick sole akin to that featured on many of its trekking and hiking styles, super chunky and leaning into a penny loafer design. And in 2009, in a collaboration with the fashion brand Telfar during New York Fashion Week, it was the Mary Jane's turn to receive a Converse update.

BELOW: All Star Pro BB.

Having been out of the game for over a decade, Converse also re-entered the basketball fold in 2019 with the release of a performance basketball shoe – the All Star Pro BB. It combined on-court experience with the latest technological advances in basketball footwear, to deliver new levels in performance as well as aesthetics.

A festive take on the All Star classic, and no doubt a design that will become highly collectible, came in 2023, when a Holiday Converse collection was themed in baked orange and Christmas-tree green colours, featuring little gingerbread men and reindeer clambering around them.

Apparel makes the brand more inclusive, which has always been a key part of the Converse identity.

Converse has also served when it comes to weddings. The Wedding Collection offers personalized Converse shoes, white or blue versions, and heels. Styles including the Chuck Taylor All Star Lift can be customized with words or slogans printed on the sole, such as 'Mr', 'Mrs', 'It was always you' and 'Forever ain't enough'. There are styles available with lace and glitter, plus the option to add extra satin or organza laces. Practical benefits include being able to dance and last throughout the whole day.

When it comes to all of these designs and styles, many highly collectible and covetable, an important question is: how does one care for Converse sneakers? According to the brand's guidelines, it is advisable not to throw them in the washing machine. Instead some mild soap and lukewarm water is suggested, using a damp cloth to gently rub the shoes, testing a section of the sneaker that is not visible first. Suede requires a suede brush.

And remember, it's not just shoes that Converse offers. You will also find T-shirts and caps, hoodies and sweatshirts, jackets and shorts, which have all contributed to Converse making inroads into lifestyle territory, rather than remaining just a sportswear brand. The apparel also makes the brand more inclusive, which has always been a key part of the Converse identity.

Basketball, skateboarding or the creative industries: which one do you most associate with Converse? The truth is, they're all relevant to the Converse world, to its branding and brand building. Brandon Avery, Converse's vice president of global innovation, who heads up the company's lab in Boston, told menswear lifestyle website Mr Porter in 2020, 'Converse has some deep roots; we have this unique connection to emotion.'

Such is Converse's genius that it has cleverly managed to straddle this trio of fields – all three of which form a unique ecosystem – to impactful effect over the years. It has achieved this through bold and provocative advertising, inclusive grassroots campaigns and a constant dialogue with its audience.

RIGHT: Sarah Jessica Parker wearing Converse while filming *Sex and the City 2* (2009).

Basketball

One of basketball's most famous sons, Larry Bird is a player from Indiana who led the Boston Celtics to three NBA championships – 1981, 1984 and 1986 – and is considered one of the greatest pure shooters of all time. He first met Magic Johnson on the court in 1979, ending that season at Indiana State University with a loss. Their rivalry would become a significant centrepiece for the rise of the NBA in the 1980s, and the story would also play out in Converse advertising.

Bird was drafted by the Celtics but didn't start to play professionally until the 1979/80 season. During the course of his career, he became known as one of the greatest players in NBA history – the Celtics won their first NBA title with Bird. He was also a 12-time All Star and won three consecutive Most Valuable Player

TOP: Larry Bird of the Boston Celtics.

BOTTOM: Magic Johnson of the Los Angeles Lakers.

(MVP) awards (1984–86). Retiring from the game in 1992, he was elected to the Naismith Memorial Basketball Hall of Fame in 1998.

Magic Johnson, meanwhile, his rival and Converse campaign co-star, played for the LA Lakers. He had earned the name 'Magic' in high school with his creative and entertaining ball skills, and he led his school to a state championship in 1977, and Michigan State University to the National Collegiate Athletic Association championship in 1979 – where he encountered Bird. Johnson achieved great success with the Lakers and became the first rookie to win the NBA's MVP award. Named one of the greatest players in NBA history in 1996, he was also inducted into the Naismith Memorial Basketball Hall of Fame, in 2002.

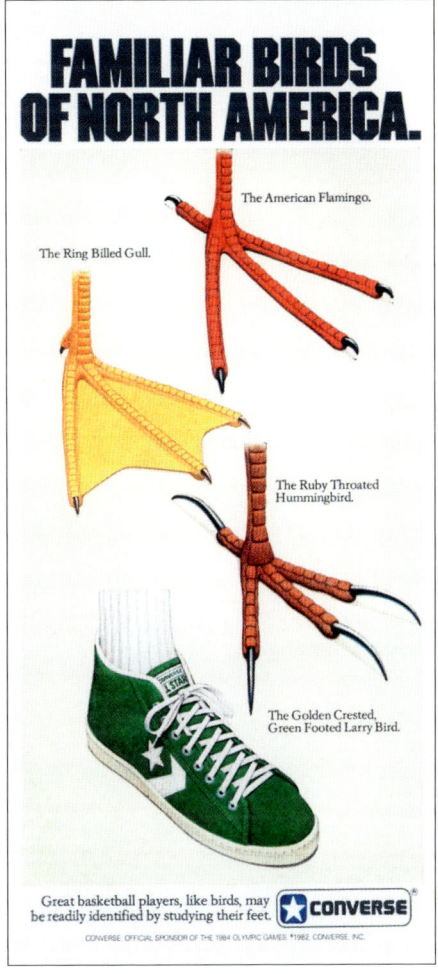

FAMILIAR BIRDS OF NORTH AMERICA.

The American Flamingo.

The Ring Billed Gull.

The Ruby Throated Hummingbird.

The Golden Crested, Green Footed Larry Bird.

Great basketball players, like birds, may be readily identified by studying their feet. **CONVERSE**®

CONVERSE: OFFICIAL SPONSOR OF THE 1984 OLYMPIC GAMES. *1982 CONVERSE, INC.

ABOVE: Advert from the 1980s, referencing Larry Bird.

It was the battle between Johnson/the Lakers and Bird/the Celtics to win the league that put basketball front and centre in the 1980s and spurred a new chapter of fandom and interest in the NBA. At the time, part of Converse's marketing strategy had been to kit out the league's best players. Their famous advertising campaign for the Converse Weapon, featuring the tagline 'Choose Your Weapon', pitted Bird and Johnson against one another to provocative effect (see page 81). The advert received an update following the shoe's re-release, followed by a new campaign fronted by Shai Gilgeous-Alexander (see pages 68–69), which read, perhaps with intended irony, 'Create history not hype'.

Before Michael Jordan signed with Nike, the NBA star wore Converse on the court, and during the 1983 Pan-American games he played for Team USA wearing a pair of All Stars. That same pair went up for auction in 2023, selling for US$37,668. It was not the first time his shoes have hit the auction block: In 2017, a pair of his game-worn sneakers set a record at the time, selling for US$190,373. The shoes were said to have been worn by Jordan in the gold medal game against Spain at the 1984 LA Olympics; they were autographed and included his orthotic inserts. They were also considered to be the last pair Jordan wore in a game as an amateur, as well as the last time he wore Converse in an official game.

RIGHT: Shai Gilgeous-Alexander holding a Converse Weapon in 2024.

However, the brand has found more famous faces to front its basketball leanings, and Shai Gilgeous-Alexander is the newest Converse star. The Oklahoma City Thunder player became the face of the Converse Weapon re-launch in early 2024, having already established something of a partnership with the brand in the summer of 2020. He joined the Converse family as a 21-year-old rising star, and is now on board to bring the brand's basketball prowess back to the future.

'The underdog mentality that the brand has and that I've had my whole career,' Gilgeous-Alexander said in 2024, 'our stories kind of align with that. We have the same vision for the future of Converse basketball.' Speaking to ESPN in 2020, he also explained that 'The exclusiveness of the brand, not having so many guys, and the ability to express myself on and off the court in so many different ways appeals to me so much.'

In 2024 the star player was given the title of Creative Director of Converse Basketball. The brand said it was proud to strengthen its relationship with the NBA All Star, and 'Together, Shai and Converse will bring a hands-on approach to the creation, execution, and overall aesthetic of his collections, which will provide a new style-driven perspective, taking inspiration from various aspects of his life.'

A clever project in 2023 built on all of this basketball history, harking back to Converse's origins as a popular footwear choice for college players. The Chuck Taylor Custom College Collection was geared towards March Madness, the basketball games that take place between colleges annually each spring. The classic style meant that fans could support their team with their own designs – the canvas uppers could be coloured in their college colours, including the heel strip, tongue, lining and stitching, as well as the embroidered text along the heel strip – and the college mascot or logo could then go on the ankle. It was a full-circle kind of moment.

Converse can be counted among the sneakers that helped define skateboarding.

Skateboarding

Over the past 20 years, Converse has recreated and evolved many of its iconic styles especially for skateboarding – with the originals thought to have been adopted by skateboarders during the 1970s and 1980s. Today, models include the AS-1 Pro, the One Star Pro, Louie Lopez Pro and CTAS Pro.

Converse can certainly be counted among the sneakers that helped define skateboarding, alongside Vans, Air Jordan and Airwalk. Sneaker Freaker sums up the appeal of Converse as follows:

'Skaters loved Chucks for their cheap price, thin and grippy vulcanized rubber sole that provided a great board feel, and the signature toecap that protected toes and enhanced durability.'

Converse introduced its CONS skate programme in 2009, which consists of a group of skateboarding ambassadors who promote the sport with tours and demos, helping to cement the brand as a backbone of the skating world. The CONS team today includes skaters Kenny Anderson, Louie Lopez and Zered Bassett, who have promoted the One Star sneaker around the world.

For the 2024 Olympic Games, the Brooklyn-based CONS team rider Alexis Sablone designed the skateboarding federation kits for the American and Japanese teams. Sablone, a former Olympian, said, 'It never crossed my mind that I'd get to design federation kits. Then again, there was a point when I didn't even think skate would be an Olympic sport.' The AS-1 Pro was her signature skateboarding shoe for Converse, crafted to be 'methodically destroyed'. She has also worked on apparel, and frequently designs sneakers as part of the Converse Create Next collection.

In 2023, the Design Museum in London hosted an exhibition called 'Skateboard', developed in partnership with Converse, which documented the history of skateboard design from the 1950s through

LEFT: A skate ramp at the 'Skateboard' exhibition at London's Design Museum.

to the present day. Said to be the first UK exhibition to explore the evolution of skateboard design in such detail, it showcased innovative skateboards, including one belonging to the legendary Tony Hawk, and looked at how skateboarding had taken off. What is noteworthy is that this seminal exhibition was done in conjunction with Converse and not one of the other legacy skate brands, which goes to show just how far the brand has evolved.

Creatives

From the Rolling Stones to Iggy Pop and Lady Gaga to Gigi Hadid, the brand has found itself on the feet of some of the world's most original tastemakers throughout the years. It boasts a rich heritage of creatives who have found their style, personality or unique identity expertly expressed by wearing a pair of Converse sneakers. As it began to emerge, this new fanbase seemed to shake up the wholesome brand and appeared to enjoy the rebellious, anti-capitalist sentiment expressed by its relatively inexpensive shoes.

'The All Star becomes a part of culture in ways that Converse had never really originally intended,' said the sneaker author and creative director Elizabeth Semmelhack. 'It goes on to have meaning in many different realms outside of basketball.' This is

RIGHT: The Sex Pistols in London in 1976.

something she in part puts down to it having an authenticity or a 'rawness' that has not only endured in terms of the design, but also has managed, from a branding point of view, to hop across the genres. 'It's remarkable that somebody can continue to wear a basic design and not look like you're dressing up in your great-great-grandfather's clothes,' she adds. The literal blank canvas has enabled the brand to grow and become a classic.

Once upon a time, Converse's closest association was with basketball, but in contemporary culture it is with subversion: punks, skaters and musicians are now its default, and convey the alternative sensibilities with which the brand has become associated and which are now the currency of cool, taking the place once held by sport. The Sex Pistols and the Ramones have

LEFT: Madonna performing in London in 2012 wearing Converse.

been among the more confrontational of Converse wearers; Tommy Ramone was reported to have said that he didn't really know who Chuck Taylor was – he doesn't seem to have cared either, going so far as to call the shoes 'cheap'.

The Converse All Stars programme builds on this creative legacy and provides a platform for emerging global creatives – 'those who are independent enough not to follow, shaping what's next, and creating their own terms,' according to the brand. The programme is active in 33 cities around the world, and champions change in both sport and culture, giving successful applicants access to events and networking opportunities as well as resources and potential funding. Current All Stars members include Altay, a filmmaker from Turkey; Poonpun, an illustrator from Thailand; Polish musician Wiktoria; and Navinder, a London fashion designer. This all chimes with recent campaigns featuring the likes of Billie Eilish, who created a range of Converse embellished with her song lyrics, and which could be customized by the wearer. She wore hers while performing on *Saturday Night Live* in 2024.

LEFT: Billie Eilish, Converse fan and collaborator.

Advertising

Converse has never shied away from advertising their wares, and some of the early campaigns, from the 1930s through to the 1960s, with their nostalgic graphics and all-American feel, are among the most visually interesting (see page 80, top left). Illustrations of the shoes are shown up-close, with a complimentary background colour, and wording is self-assured. One 1953 advert notes that there are 'Two Leaders', and shows the Chuck Taylor All Star in both canvas and leather.

In 1968, the confident messaging is, 'In basketball there is only one All Star', depicting a pair of the high tops propped on top of one another in the foreground, the spotlight squarely on them, with the basketball court behind. A 1973 ad quotes a statistic, stating that '8 out of 10 players in every major college and junior tournament wore All Stars' that year. And in a 1976 TV commercial for the All Star, the voiceover says, 'It's easier to be on your toes and on your game when you're wearing Converse All Stars.' The camera pans to a close-up of the sneakers, which catch the light, looking a little magical and evoking a hint of nostalgia even back then. Notably, the focus is squarely on performance here, rather than using famous faces or fancy tricks.

A year later, in 1977, this strategy changed for the Converse Pro Leather: Julius 'Dr. J' Erving starred in a commercial wearing the high top. He is seen dunking, almost dancing, as the jingle sings, 'Hey, hey, Dr. J, where'd you get those moves?' and ends with, 'Where'd you get those moves, are you wearing magic shoes?' as he flies high into the air. The accompanying print ad reads, 'Hey, Dr. J, How'd you get there?' and shows the player about to make a slam dunk. The inference is clear: Converse make you superhuman. A later print ad from 1984 simply states, 'Just what the doctor ordered', with Dr. J's face shown below the new biomechanically engineered Converse Star Tech.

One 1953 advert notes that there are 'Two Leaders', and shows the Chuck Taylor All Star in both canvas and leather.

From 1984, the tagline 'It's like a jungle out there' plays on the idea of the All Star being the 'most hunted canvas shoe around', which is fun and clever, if not a little surreal (see page 31). As is the mid-80s 'Limousines for your feet' ad, which appeals to 'people who want to go places in style' and shows a giant pair 'parked' outside New York's Plaza Hotel, in a witty moment that points to the brand's strong personality (see page 80, bottom). In another witty moment, the Batman logo in 1989 promotes the reintroduction of wingtips (see page 82, bottom right), and shows Converse managing to tap into the cultural references of the time to highlight its

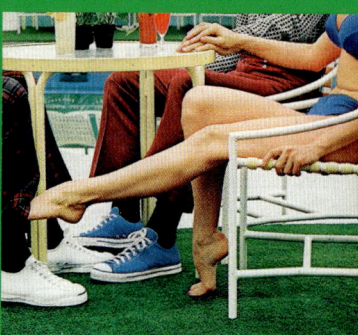

CLOCKWISE FROM LEFT: Converse adverts from 1961, 1973, 1986 and 1985.

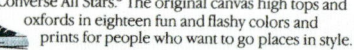

CHOOSE YOUR WEAPON.

Larry Bird and Magic Johnson. When they play, they push themselves to the limit. And they trust their performance to Converse. The shoe they choose to do battle in is the Converse® Weapon™— a shoe biomechanically designed to help players play their best.

These shoes offer superior traction because of their natural rubber outsoles. They're incredibly cushioned as well, due to the Center of Pressure outsole and a shock absorbing EVA midsole. And for the strong ankle support that Bird, Magic and every other ballplayer needs, there's the unique Y-Bar Ankle Support System.

Besides all these features, the Converse Weapon has a comfortable, removable insole and an extra padded collar that combines with the Y-Bar System for enhanced ankle support and comfort. Bird and Magic have chosen their weapons. Now choose yours.

The Converse Weapon. One more reason why athletes like Bird and Magic depend on Converse for the best possible performance.

THE CONVERSE® WEAPONS™

CONVERSE
Reach for the stars.

©1986 Converse, Inc.

RUN!

CLOCKWISE FROM LEFT:
Converse adverts from 1988,
2007, 2004, 1989 and 1991.

GET CHUCKED

CONVERSE
by JOHN VARVATOS
CLOTHES AND SHOES FOR GUYS AND GIRLS

I'm Ray. Born and raised a suburban boy. Side street. White house. **CONVERSE**
Green shutters. Ever since I was six, I played basketball. My three   It's what's inside that counts.
brothers and I played year-round in the ... driveway. Dad never had to worry
about shoveling snow. We would ... already be out there shooting
around. My very first pair of ... ball shoes were
the Converse Chuck ... Taylor All
Star® ("Chucks." ... As were
my second. I ... played in
church leagues. In school. ... Summer
leagues. In school. ... after school.
And I ... always liked
... the game. ... Maybe
... it's because
it was the one ... thing I
was really good at. ... after high school
I worked a bunch ... of different jobs.
Finally I took one at ... Covenant House in
Manhattan counsel ... adolescents who'd
run into trouble. (Or ... be run away from it.)
At times, the job ca ... brutal. But on those
days when a kid ... back to visit, it's
very rewarding. I ... like my job. It's
also great livin ... City. Bounc ...
a ball four time ... sudden ... ou
have a pick ... game ... Only
it's not the suburb ... zon ... efense,
jump-shot game. ... N ... it's the
man-to-man, tak ... it-to-the-
hoop, no-foul ... nless-you-
see-blood game ... ccasionally
I hit the court wit ... latest pair
of Cons® Chuck ... ... because we
still make a pre ... ex ... d pair.

ALL ★ STAR
MADE IN U.S.A.

CONVERSE REINTRODUCES WINGTIPS.

They're back. Batman® and his arch enemy, the Joker.™ From Converse. At select stores for a
limited time only. Call 1-800-545-4323 for the store nearest you.

★ CONVERSE®

www.grouperoyer.com

own relevance (it had produced Joker and Batman logo print sneakers). A 1950s shot of the iconic James Dean looking especially cool featured in an advert promoting Jack Purcells in 1989, depicting a classic and sophisticated way of showcasing the brand.

Meanwhile, Converse's 80s' running shoe adverts play with language around marathons and endurance (remember, this is the performance era), such as 'Avoid breakdowns on the road'. Other straplines that have made an impact include 'It's what's inside that counts', a series featuring former power forward for the New York Knicks Larry Johnson, and 'The winningest pair', which was actually a tennis shoe advert.

The brand has consistently fostered an association with strength and success.

In 1984, when the Star Tech was the official athletics shoe of the Olympics, a Converse commercial showed a young boy dreaming about dribbling a basketball, waking up, taking a shower, then grabbing a snack and hitting the streets of New York City. The tagline reads: 'To dribble from New York to L.A., you've gotta have a dream.' The young star is dressed in a similar way to the fictional film characters Ferris Bueller and Marty McFly, who we also see wearing Converse in starring roles later that decade.

The brand has consistently fostered an association with strength and success, as is demonstrated with 1986's 'Choose Your Weapon' ad, which pictures Bird and Johnson standing back-to-back, each holding up their Converse Weapon in team colours. The rivals are pitched as going one-on-one, armed with their performance 'weapon' of choice (see page 81). The TV ad features six NBA players, including Bird and Johnson, who rap about how the high tops improve their performance on the court. It ends with Bird saying, 'You already know what they did for me, I walked away with the MVP.' It is perhaps on the cheesier side of Converse's advertising, yet conveys just how dominant a role Converse the brand played during its NBA days. A later 1987 advert informs us that 'more and more of the NBA's big guns are wielding a new weapon', in reference to the famous shoe.

And so into the nineties, when Golden State Warriors shooting guard Latrell Sprewell star in the 1995 Acropolis commercial: 'This man owns so much court, we call him the Landlord', is how it begins. He is then complimented on his sneakers and replies, 'Cons, baby', interspersed with shots of on-court action. It's a bolder, more direct form of advertising, and feels very of its time.

Dennis Rodman starred in a 1997 commercial for Converse to promote the All Star Rodman, one of his signature shoes with the brand, which was apparently inspired by his tattoos. Rodman asks the viewer, 'Maybe if I didn't have tattoos or piercings, or dye my hair – maybe if I didn't think for myself, or be myself – would you see me then?' The ad has a jagged, subversive feel, but still invokes the brand's fundamental message of prizing individuality.

Following its sale to Nike in the early 2000s, and a step away from the basketball court for a time, Converse has become better known for its cultural collaborations than its advertising campaigns as a way of spreading the word (see Chapter 6).

In 2024, Charli XCX officially became part of the Converse family. The singer commenced her relationship with the brand by starring in a holiday campaign, celebrating her love of the Chuck Taylor All Star, photographed by Sharna Osborne. In a statement reported by Footwear News, she said, 'I wear my Chucks so much they have holes in them, so I was really excited to work with Converse so I could get a new pair,' adding, 'they're iconic'.

RIGHT: Charli XCX became a Converse ambassador in 2024.

Logo

Aside from an underlying sense of cool – which can move with whatever is in fashion, be it basketball or grunge – the thing that truly brings the brand together is the Converse logo: the distinctive ankle patch, the chevron and the star, and the vintage Converse All Star heel plate – sometimes used all at once on one shoe.

Unlike Nike's famous logo-creation story, there is little information to be found about the making of the Converse logo. Jim Labadini, an employee of the company, seems to be given credit for some of it in certain corners of the internet. And of course we know that Chuck Taylor did his part to make that ankle patch recognizable with his own name. Yet if you see the star or the chevron, you instantly know it's Converse. The star is almost like the twinkle in one's eye, recalling that all-American retro charm. The chevron provides a sense of movement, which has always been part of the brand's DNA, from running to playing ball to making change in creative fields.

In 2017, The Drum, an online news site for the marketing and media industries, reported a subtle change in the logo, which it claimed even devoted sneakerheads might not have noticed. It pointed out that the star was still part of the logo, but it was now butted up against a chevron, with the brand name appearing beneath both of them.

The Drum also reported Converse's vice president of global brand design, Adam Cohn, as saying; 'The star chevron has been in use since the 70s and we wanted to make it a major part of our identity – that part of the brief was clear: let's leverage an icon that's part of our heritage that's also representative of moving forward. The challenge was getting our name in the mix, so we had to develop a new wordmark.' A wordmark is a logo design using a text-only statement to brand a product. The creative team looked at logos dating back to the Converse Rubber Shoe Company in the 1920s and 1930s and discovered that, 'The "Converse" word has been written in many different ways as a logo over time; in the end it was about mining details.' Cohn also said that the Chuck Taylor logo would remain intact.

When you start to look, you'll see Converse everywhere: on the student in their first year at university; the lead singer in the latest band (or the lead singer in an already famous band); your favourite scene from your favourite film; in the TV show you're currently streaming. Converse, from its classic and cool American roots, really has managed to permeate all aspects of popular culture.

It's not that celebrities wearing a brand is the (only) measure of cultural cool, but it should be pointed out that the list of celebrities who have worn Converse, particularly Chuck Taylors, is endless and impressive. To name but a few: Willow Smith, Janet Jackson, Ryan Reynolds, Kim Kardashian, Sarah Jessica Parker, Emma Roberts, Kaia Gerber, Alexa Chung, Gwyneth Paltrow, Joaquin Phoenix and Rihanna. Just recently, *The Bear* star Ebon Moss-Bachrach was spotted out and about in New York wearing his. He is just one of many; such downtime sightings are a common occurrence. Simply put, it's cool to wear Converse.

RIGHT: Shabba Doo (wearing Converse) with Lucinda Dickey in *Breakin'/ Breakdance* (1984).

Politics

Among the many celebrities and people in positions of power who wear Converse, there are some significant and surprising examples. US politician Kamala Harris famously sparked the 'Chucks and pearls' trend while out on the campaign trail with President Joe Biden in 2020. Harris regularly wears pearls in honour of her university sorority, Alpha Kappa Alpha (members are known as 'pearls'), and she is also a fan of Converse All Stars. Leading up to Inauguration Day, various Facebook groups urged women to pay tribute to the new Vice President by wearing pearls, further spreading the trend – to the extent that some began to refer to the occasion as 'Chucks and Pearls Day'. Back on her own presidential campaign trail in 2024, Harris reprised the look.

Harris told online New York magazine The Cut that she has a whole collection of Chuck Taylors in a variety of different colours, fabrics and for different occasions, which she reeled off. In a story in the *Guardian* newspaper in 2020, commentators explored the significance of her wearing the shoes, which included showing she was prepared to roll up her sleeves, ready for action; that they conveyed an authenticity and approachability; and that they also appealed to a younger audience.

RIGHT: Kamala Harris wore Converse for her 2020 and 2024 political campaigns.

The former VP also wore her Converse on another important occasion: when featuring on the front cover of *American Vogue*, which has long been seen as a cultural landmark and therefore represented an opportunity of great significance. For the February cover in 2021, she appeared wearing a blazer by Donald Deal, black trousers, a white T-shirt and dark Converse sneakers. The famous US fashion magazine is known for its glossy covers, upon which designer heels are usually worn, or if they are not then it's because it's a barefoot beach or swim scene. This instance marked a particularly mainstream cultural crossover, as well as a historic moment for Converse. There was some controversy around this image and a further digital cover was released. Regardless of the politics though, it was an important milestone for Converse..

Red Carpet

It might be less surprising to find out that man-of-the-moment Timothée Chalamet is a Converse fan. The American–French actor has been praised for his fashion sense ever since he appeared on style radars back in 2017. Things ramped up in 2019 when he wore a silver Haider Ackermann suit to the premiere of his movie *The King*, and then a backless halter ensemble to the premiere of *Bones and All*.

RIGHT: Timothée Chalamet at the 2021 Met Gala.

Such were his mounting style credentials that Chalamet became the co-chair of the fashion industry's equivalent of the Oscars, the Met Gala, in 2021 (alongside Billie Eilish, Amanda Gorman and Naomi Osaka). This might not be surprising, but what he wore to the event – which he reportedly walked ten blocks to attend – was. Finishing off his all-white satin tuxedo with black lapels and white sweats, once again by Haider Ackermann, was a pair of Converse, which grounded the slightly off-beat and futuristic look, keeping it in the here and now and signifying that this was a young actor on the ascent.

The themes of the Met Gala typically invite the weird and the wonderful in terms of dressing up, with some guests choosing to be more adventurous than others. For 2021, the theme was 'In America: A Lexicon of Fashion', so Converse was an especially appropriate choice, given its all-American heritage – from its early basketball days to cementing its status as a firm fixture on the red carpet.

Although that was not always the case. Today, to wear Converse on the red carpet is to bring a bit of humanity to your outfit and convey personality, charisma, fun and ease, which nods to the brand's ethos of encouraging personal expression and

LEFT: Millie Bobby Brown at the 2018 SAG Awards.

offering something for everyone. All Stars, high or low, give the impression that a celebrity is perhaps more down to earth and unafraid of disrupting the formal dress codes that have long been established in Hollywood. The sneakers enable them to come across as just the right amount of rebellious and anti-establishment, without being too confrontational about it.

The actress Kristen Stewart has memorably worn Converse on the red carpet and at events numerous times, often paired with dresses or outfits that, in a formal sense, might have commanded a heel (she has also been known to ditch the heels part way through and put on her kicks). At the MTV Movie Awards in 2009, she wore a low top pair of Converse with a Yigal Azrouël black and red dress. It was a move that earned her many a fashion salute. The shoes have become a badge of subversion, a way to add edge and convey alternative style.

Fashion

As renegade and purposefully jarring as they can appear, Converse sneakers have a talent for seeming effortless and cool. During fashion weeks, models click away on their phones backstage while waiting for makeup, often slouched on the floor and wearing Converse. They hop on the backs of

RIGHT: Kristen Stewart at the 2009 MTV Movie Awards.

motorbikes heading off to their next casting or show wearing Converse. And they are captured by street-style photographers looking off-duty yet put-together in Converse. All of this is instrumental in heightening the shoes' fashion appeal. Regularly seen wearing her navy high tops with an ethereal dress or a printed floral skirt, jumper and petite handbag, British tastemaker and fashion darling Alexa Chung is also a fan.

Among the models most often spotted wearing Converse sneakers is Kaia Gerber, the daughter of one of the original supermodels, Cindy Crawford. 'Gerber is the only consistent sports shoe wearer: the 18-year-old lives in her Converse hi-tops', wrote *British Vogue* in 2020, noting that despite the very many colour options available, the model rarely strays from black; teamed with trousers, with skirts, looking smart and looking casual. The fashion publication continued: 'The timeless lace-ups underline the *British Vogue* cover star's preppy aesthetic. Boxy blazers or leather jackets, straight-leg jeans and Chucks are the pillars of her off-duty uniform, which has hardly deviated since she rose to fame.' In summer, Gerber might team them with printed skirts or cut-offs, or head to the gym in them: 'the joy of All Stars is that they make for a failsafe blank canvas.'

LEFT: Kaia Gerber wearing Converse in New York in 2029.

LEFT: Kurt Cobain of
Nirvana in Converse
in 1990.

Music

British and American punk icons the Sex Pistols and the Ramones have famously worn Converses sneakers – the latter supposedly not really caring about anything other than that they were 'cheap'. Nirvana's Kurt Cobain (see pages 102–03) was among the key protagonists of the grunge movement of the 1990s, and his plaid shirts, cosy cardigans and semi-baggy jeans were often anchored by a pair of Converse. In 2008, 14 years after his death, Converse debuted the Kurt Cobain collection, which featured designs decorated with artwork and scribbles taken from his personal notebooks. Cobain was often pictured wearing Chuck Taylor All Stars, Jack Purcells or One Stars, and the collection included all three styles with frayed details as well as the musician's signature embroidered on the outer. They were priced between US$50 and $65.

Converse's presence in music has stretched far and wide across eras and genres. They were, and still are, a mainstay in the wardrobe of Avril Lavigne, the Canadian singer who rose to fame in the early noughties as a rebellious teen. Lavigne rode the edge of the emo wave and what would become indie sleaze but did it with a feminist kick: think torn fishnets, loosely worn ties, kohl-rimmed eyes, skater chains and – of course – a pair of Converse.

RIGHT: Avril Lavigne performing in Atlanta, Georgia, in 2002 wearing Converse.

In the early noughties, this Blink-182 style was in vogue; girls wore band T-shirts with retro dresses and added a pair of Converse. The look was a kind of reprieve of *Wayne's World* for the post-millennium world. The aesthetic was epitomized by Jack and Kelly Osbourne in reality TV show *The Osbournes*, featuring the real lives of eccentric metal head Ozzie Osbourne and his family (Ozzie is also a fan, and was involved in Black Sabbath collabs with Converse in 2008 and 2014).

Converse sneakers also became a part of the scruffy but cool uniform of the noughties band The Strokes, who are often credited with changing the way men dressed in this decade. Founded in New York in 1998, the band's style arguably had similarities with local heroes the Ramones. While music movements such as nu metal were reaching their peak just before the millennium, with chunkier sneakers such as Vans and Etnies in the picture, The Strokes went the other way – skinny jeans and skinny ties, with leather jackets and, always, Converse.

In 2001 The Strokes launched their debut album *Is This It*. The back of the UK cover is shot in black and white from a low angle, showcasing their shaggy hair and Converse-clad feet. With their neat silhouettes and slim trouser profiles, along with the

RIGHT: Kelly Osbourne in Converse at the 2002 MTV Movie Awards.

iconic shoes, it looks as if they might have time-travelled from the 1950s or 1970s.

The Strokes' aesthetic was thrifted; lead singer Julian Casablancas stated that he didn't care much for clothes, but pointed out it was important to wear things that gave you social confidence. And that is something Converse seem to have been doing ever since they first stepped on court. It was Chuck Taylor who instilled this sense of self-assurance into the brand early on, and campaigns over the years have instructed Converse wearers to 'Unleash your chaos', declaring, 'Your season, your rules'.

The Strokes helped promote an effortless rock chic that saw sneakers worn with suits, adding casual to formal to make it fashion. Previously this could have come across as sloppy or unprofessional, but it now made sense as part of the indie sleaze era – an updated and more glamorous, less dark, version of grunge.

Collaborating with musicians both unofficially – as with The Strokes and the Ramones, who just happened to wear them – and officially, as with Black Sabbath, is something Converse continues to benefit from, building on yet another aspect of its scene-hopping heritage.

LEFT: The Strokes performing in New York in 2006 wearing Converse.

The American rapper Snoop Dogg often performs in Converse (donning a pair of white Chuck Taylor All Stars with thick blue laces for Hip Hop 50 Live in New York in 2023). A 2023 article in the *New York Times'* magazine *The Athletic* noted that Chucks had become a symbol of West Coast living and hip-hop by the 1990s; 'White New York had Timberlands, California had Chucks'. Californian rappers Snoop Dogg and fellow Californian rapper Ice Cube wore Chucks as they rose to prominence. And more recently, in 2023, Terrace Martin, the Californian producer and rapper, released the song 'Chucks'.

The indie sound popularized by The Strokes would be replaced by the rise of new rave, or 'nu-rave', yet Converse was still along for the ride, transitioning from the look associated with the jolly angst rock of the new century into pops of neon that ushered in a new style era. English rock band the Klaxons, synonymous with new rave, wore skinny jeans, loud tees and could be clocked in bashed-up Converse. The style was a riff on the colour-clash brights of the 1980s, and girls wore leggings, beads and unlaced Converse. While designer sneakers like those by Dior and Chanel would have a moment in the early 2010s, after new rave, from around 2008, there would be a general penchant for heels once more in fashion.

RIGHT: Snoop Dogg performing in New York in 2004 wearing Converse.

Film and TV

In a 2021 round-up of iconic moments featuring Converse in film and TV history, French fashion magazine *L'Officiel* highlighted Sofia Coppola's *Marie Antoinette* (2006). Their appearance in the film has been thought of by some, incorrectly, as a 'goof'. The internet movie site IMDb, however, clarified that the pair of pastel-blue Converse, though clearly anachronistic, was meant to convey that 'despite the era, her being of royal blood, and immensely tasked with performing her duty to continue the royal bloodline, Marie Antoinette was still a teenage girl who was trying to find her place in the world.' It made perfect sense and it was a clever styling trick.

Retrospectively, the timeless quality of the sneakers also makes sense for the time-travelling Marty McFly in *Back to the Future* (1985), who spends time in the 1950s and the 1980s – notable periods in sneaker culture. There is perhaps no shoe that feels more at home across the decades than the Converse All Star.

Other notable film and TV moments that get name-checked in *L'Officiel*'s editorial include *Rocky* (1976), *The Outsiders* (1983), *The Breakfast Club* (1985), *Stand By Me* (1986), *The Basketball Diaries*

RIGHT: John Travolta in *Grease* (1978).

ABOVE: Daniel
Radcliffe in *Harry
Potter and the
Half-Blood
Prince* (2009).

(1995), *Trainspotting* (1996), the *Harry Potter*
movies (2001–11) and *Stranger Things* (2016). And
there are hundreds more. Superfan Hal Peterson
has logged 1,109 Converse film appearances on his
website the ChucksConnection, worn by everyone
from Jamie Lee Curtis and John Cusack to Kate
Winslet and Christopher Walken.

Off-screen, film has had an influence on the shoes in
turn. In December 2023, to coincide with the release
of the *Wonka* film starring Timothée Chalamet (who,
as we know, is a big Converse fan), Converse

announced a Wonka-themed collaboration featuring its Chuck 70, Chuck Taylor All Star and All Star BB Trilliant CX shoes. The range was suitably sweet in colourways including 'Chocolate Swirl' and 'Oompa Loompa', and apparel was also available. It felt like a fitting collaboration given that walking into a Converse store is like walking into the footwear version of a candy store, with so many colours, prints and styles to make one's mouth water.

In 2022, *Star Wars* actor John Boyega told *British Vogue* that he had his older sister to thank for his first

PAGE 116: River Phoenix in *Stand By Me* (1986).

PAGE 117: Mark Wahlberg and Leonardo DiCaprio in *The Basketball Diaries* (1995).

pair of Converse: 'There was a nice moment when we were both a size seven,' he revealed, sharing a story of the high tops he inherited as a teenager. 'From then on, I've always been rocking them and following the culture.' Boyega joined the brand's All Stars programme as a mentor in 2021, as part of its Create Next Film Project to foster the work of five Black filmmakers from London. The community-focused project awarded funding to Ade Femzo, Kaylen Francis, Kemi Anna Adeeko, Lorraine Khamali and Ibrahim Muhammad to make a five-minute short film, and they received guidance throughout

ABOVE: Ewan McGregor in *Trainspotting* (1996).

the six-month process. *British Vogue* said that he hoped the collaboration with Converse would serve 'not as a moment, but a movement; that it creates a ricochet effect, prompting other brands to follow suit by pouring time and resources into something with impact far beyond a marketing campaign.'

When 'normcore' peaked on the fashion scene in 2015, bolstered by the Demna and Guram Gvasalia-founded brand Vetements, there was a sudden focus on streetwear – beyond the brands who typically specialized in it – leading to collaborations across

BELOW: Patrick J. Adams in *Suits* (2011-19).

the sportswear and high-fashion industries. Meanwhile, the 2020 Covid pandemic encouraged us all to wear sneakers again, and a host of TV characters has made us dig back into our closets – not least, the stars of Netflix's 1980s-nostalgia-heavy sci-fi hit *Stranger Things*, and Rue, played by Zendaya, in HBO's edgy teen-drama *Euphoria*. Zendaya's costume comprises board shorts, baggy T-shirts and Converse. In an interview with *Vogue Australia* in 2022, Zendaya talked about her Chuck Taylors, and how they had a sort of power: 'I have a superstitious thing with

BELOW: Zendaya in *Euphoria* (2019–22).

my shoes,' she explained. 'Those are still the same shoes from season one. They're falling apart, the laces have broken, like, so many times . . . they're barely holding on, but I will not change them.' Indeed – like so many of the die-hard Converse community.

ABOVE: Blake Anderson (right) wearing Converse in *Workaholics* (2011–17).

Future

As we've discussed previously, one of the great appeals of the Converse sneaker is that it is timeless. In an incredibly techy and overdesigned sports shoe market, Converse's designs have remained among the most analogue of all (notable collaborations aside). But that is not to say that Converse is not a part of the digital world, or the future of sneakers.

In 2022, the brand joined with Snapchat to launch a Bitmoji capsule as part of the latest 'outfit sharing' feature in the app. Since Covid, there has been significant growth in digital fashion, meaning fashion that can be 'worn' in the virtual world – be that social media avatars or skins in video games. Converse supplied a wardrobe for users, which included Chuck Taylor All Stars, chevron tees, shorts and hoodies. A further element to the digital partnership was realized IRL: physical pairs of the Lugged 2.0 shoe were released, which meant users could in turn resemble their Bitmoji icons.

In recent years, there has been much talk about sneakers and style tribes. Adidas's Sambas were so hot it hurt for a moment, and then they fell out of fashion. Cue the return of Converse – though it wasn't so much the return of the shoes as it was them flying in the face of what was now considered too mainstream (true to the brand's ethos).

Timothée Chalamet was among those leading the pack, along with Stella Maxwell and Tyler, The Creator, who became a champion when he began a Golf Le Fleur collaboration with the brand back in 2018, which focused on the Chuck Taylor All Star and Chuck 70. Tyler's latest collaboration draws on his love of dogs, specifically Airedale Terriers, for a new five-shoe collection (they are very cute).

Having been featured in what feels like every TV show and cult or commercial film over the years, it is no wonder that there is an elasticity to the Converse brand. This has made it the ideal partner when it comes to collaborations, and the brand says it drops new ones each month. In summary, as *American Vogue* wrote in 2023, 'if you're feeling uninspired by your current options, break out a pair of Chuck Taylors,' adding, 'there's a pair of Converse sneakers out there for everybody.' They are not wrong.

Collaborations

Collaborations have increasingly become a key part of fashion, enabling brands to enhance each other's credentials and access new audience streams. It's something that Converse has been engaging in to great effect for years, given that their shoes, with their relatively simple designs, lend themselves so well to providing a creative blank slate. Converse regularly releases new collaborations across a range of different categories, from high fashion to popular culture, and from celebrity endorsements and media alliances to partnerships with cutting-edge designers and cool streetwear brands.

Some of the names that have worked with the brand include: Mita Sneakers, Offspring, Number Nine, Andy Warhol, AC/DC, Superman, Despicable Me, N.Hoolywood, Dungeons and Dragons, Liverpool FC, G-Shock, Awake NY, Golf Wang, Hello Kitty, Sky High Farm Universe, BoTT, Patta, Nissin Foods, Ader Error, Clot, Pride, Peanuts, Pokemon, Slam Jam, Jean-Michel Basquiat, Transformers, John Elliott, Todd Snyder and Issa Rae.

RIGHT: Feng Chen Wang menswear Spring/ Summer fashion show, 2019, New York.

JW Anderson

Jonathan Anderson told *British Vogue* in 2019, 'I love working with the Chuck Taylor; it's a shoe I have been wearing for as long as I can remember.' In 2017, he embarked upon a long-term collaboration that was first previewed on the Pitti menswear catwalk in Milan: the Chuck Taylor All Star high tops were covered in blocks of coloured glitter on one side. When released, there were also logoed versions. In a statement, Anderson said, 'From my very first pair, Converse have represented such a radical movement in style and culture. The contrasts and similarities between the world of Converse and the world of JW Anderson creates a space of culture tension that's a dream to play within as a designer.'

The second instalment of the collaboration came in 2018 and focused on the Thunderbolt and the Chuck 70, introducing denim and suede versions; and there was more to come. 'JW Anderson for Converse has become one of the industry's most interesting collaborations,' wrote Naomi Pike for *British Vogue* in 2019. This time, the designer took the shoe and reimagined it with a jagged rubber sole for a heightened platform: the Run Star Hike was, he said, made with everyone in mind, and was styled at his show that September with summer dresses.

Anderson has said that one of the reasons he especially enjoys working with Converse is because it provides more people with access to

ABOVE: JW Anderson x Converse.

the JW Anderson brand, and he likes to be 'in touch with the Converse fan'. To celebrate the Chuck 70 'Toy' collection that the designer created for Converse in 2018, the two brands opened up a joint retail space in London's Soho. Anderson's Chucks switched out the canvas for patent vinyl and used terry towelling for the laces. 'There was something I really liked about the collaboration being just bizarre,' said Anderson, who has secured a reputation for his avant-garde and artful designs in his role as creative director at Loewe as well as with his own label.

> *Take a look at the bows at the end of catwalk shows and you will see a whole host of designers wearing Converse.*

The designer has explained that 'When you have a product which is so iconic, it forces you to be focused, because there is a parameter you have to remain within.' He has also confessed that he lives in Converse himself, and he is not the only one: take a look at the bows at the end of catwalk shows and you will see a whole host of designers wearing Converse.

LEFT: Run Star Hike, by JW Anderson for Converse.

Missoni

In 2009, *British Vogue* reported that at the Missoni menswear show in Milan, 'the fashion pack was treated to more than just Angela Missoni's answer to Spring/Summer 2010; they were also the first to see the fruit of the brand's new collaboration with Converse.' Since then, Missoni and Converse have collaborated often. It is in many ways an ideal partnership, as both are known for their signature use of the chevron – the Italian fashion house in its legendary knitwear and Converse in its logos. Here, the two blend to great effect.

Today, you will find Converse's Missoni collaborations listed on luxury resale sites such as Vestiaire Collective. It shouldn't come as a surprise. The demand for original issues has boomed in recent years as converns over sustainability and environmental issues have increasingly gripped the fashion industry – and the world at large. Missoni x Converse, as *GQ* declared in 2015, is 'one of the original high-fashion-meets-streetwear collaborations'.

When one Missoni x Converse collaboration debuted in 2014, it permeated a base beyond sneakerheads, and a *Glamour* magazine headline declared: 'Why the Missoni x Converse launch just might be the best investment buy of the season.' For a collection in 2015, having previously used the Chuck Taylor All Star and Jack Purcell silhouettes, this time Missoni

ABOVE: Missoni x Converse.

worked with Converse's Deck Star Slip 67, 'a rarely seen skate shoe shape that we'd almost forgotten about', according to *GQ*. The result was incredibly chic, somewhere between a slipper and a skate shoe. More familiar, perhaps, is the Converse Chuck Taylor All Star x Missoni 'Hiker', which first debuted at Missoni's Autumn/Winter 2016 show, and the Chuck Taylor All Star Hi x Missoni in rainbow colours from 2017.

Comme des Garçons

'History was made in 2009,' declared fashion photographer Nick Knight's SHOWstudio platform, 'when PLAY Comme des Garçons and Converse

announced their first collaboration.' It was, it said, 'a merger of streetwear and avant-garde fashion like never before'.

Comme des Garçons is the renowned conceptual, and slightly intellectual, fashion brand set up by Rei Kawakubo, known for its deconstructionist aesthetic, which came to the fore in the 1980s. Converse's initial partnership with Comme des Garçons dates back to 2006, when Kawakubo styled Chuck Taylor All Stars in her runway presentation.

Officially, though, collaboration between the brands began in 2009, when the first Converse x Comme des Garçons PLAY collection was released. It featured a joyful logo of a heart with eyes, designed by the Polish artist Filip Pagowski, and utilized the Chuck Taylor All Star silhouette. According to Converse, the teams stripped back the iconic markings of the sneaker in a bid to simplify the heritage and make it a little quirkier.

In 2015, a fourth collection was launched. It took the Chuck 70 silhouette and removed the overall minimalist feel, instead playing up the heart logo on the canvas upper. The introduction of three new colours came in 2020: vibrant green, pink and blue – which brought a softer and more playful feel to the

LEFT: Comme des Garçons x Converse.

design. Further seasonal tones were introduced for 2021 – grey and a deeper blue. That same year, they also played around with the Jack Purcell silhouette.

A more radical design introduction in 2022 was red midsoles, which were particularly striking. The same year, now over a decade after the ongoing collaboration had begun, saw the One Star get the PLAY treatment: for this iteration, the heart sat alongside the sneaker's star logo.

It featured a joyful logo of a heart with eyes, designed by the Polish artist Filip Pagowski.

Multi-hearts featured on the Chuck 70 for 2023, which again was a very lively, fun and friendly sneaker (some sports shoes can seem austere) with lots of collector appeal. And in 2024, some 15 years after the first release, came a re-release of the original design – this time on the Chuck 70 and its Ox style. Sizes for kids were also made available.

Stüssy

When news came in 2022 that there was a new reworking of the Chuck Taylor in the pipeline, in conjunction with the 1980s-born skate brand Stüssy (which, as it happens, has also collaborated with Comme des Garçons), *GQ* declared 'The Stüssy Converse Chuck Taylor is the American Dream of

collabs'. The two brands have been working together since the early 2010s, having first teamed up for a celebratory Chuck Taylor All Star collection to mark the 35th anniversary of Stüssy in 2015. In 2016, Stüssy reimagined the Converse One Star silhouette. *GQ* further reported that each time they have collaborated the sneakers have sold out.

ABOVE: Rick Owens x Converse.

Rick Owens

The American designer Rick Owens is no stranger to sneaker collaborations, having teamed up with Adidas and Veja as well as footwear brands Dr. Martens and Birkenstock. He has also added Converse to that list. Having admitted he's not actually a 'sneaker person', Owens started his own line of 'anti-sneaker' shoes – one pair named after the Ramones, who we know wore Converse in the same rebellious anti-flashy-sneaker kind of way.

Owens' debut Converse collection reworked the
Chuck 70 in both high- and low-top styles, called
Converse x DRKSHDW TURBODRK, featuring a triple
toecap and double shoe. A second collaboration
took on the Converse Weapon CX. There has also
been the DRKSHDW TURBOWPN, featuring

DRKSHDW branding, a chunky silhouette
and exaggerated proportions, including a
very tall tongue.

The Chuck Taylor DRKSTAR is considered to be
the most accessible of all the designs, which have
typically taken the otherworldliness for which Owens
is famed and wrapped it up in a sneaker-style shoe.

A-Cold-Wall*

In 2020, Samuel Ross, the founder and creative
director of the successful British brand A Cold Wall,
released the first drop of A-Cold-Wall* x Converse,
including the Chuck Taylor Lugged, which was
transformed into a boot via a grey makeover and
ACW*-branded rubber panelling covering the sole.

The designer told *GQ* that one of his earliest
memories of Converse was owning a pair of All Stars
aged 14: 'I was travelling to the Caribbean a lot and
took those shoes on numerous hikes. The experience
of my childhood effected this idea of changing the
All Star into something that is more hard-wearing.'

Also in 2020 came a minimalist take on the ERX 260
in grey, with a leather upper base and a branded
ankle strap. Ross explained that there had been
a focused approach to technical fabrics, and that
he wanted to add organic tones. Another release
came in the shape of the Chuck Taylor All Star boot,
rendered in nylon to make it more durable.

There have continued to be further team-ups between the two brands, and what is perhaps most striking about Ross's designs is their angular nature; they feel futuristic and lean into some of the more recent Converse design innovations such as the heel and the wedge.

Kith

In August 2024, Converse and Kith – a lifestyle brand and retail concept – came together to produce a Chuck Taylor All Star 70 Ox as part of the Kith Classics for Converse Fall 2024 line. The monogrammed designs were sleek and came in three colours: black, cream and a subdued dark green.

As with many Converse collaborators, this was not their first time. In 2020, Kith and Coca-Cola had reprised a partnership with Converse for a fifth season. The Converse Chuck 70 low top featured the Coca-Cola logo along the shoe's side in three colourways – navy, red or cream. It felt like a truly fitting throwback to retro Americana. Then, in 2021, a collaboration for Kith's tenth anniversary saw the release of the Kith logo-strewn Chuck taylor All Star 70 in black or white.

Off-White

The late Virgil Abloh had made a name for himself on the streetwear scene before being appointed as creative director for menswear at Louis Vuitton in

2018. He simultaneously ran his own very successful label Off-White, which enjoyed both cult and commercial success. A link-up with Converse therefore made perfect sense.

A link-up with Converse made perfect sense.

The brand's take on the Chuck 70 landed in 2018 and was striking for its details: the Off-White stamp, an orange zip-tie, signature black and white diagonal stripes on the midsole and the All Star logo on the ankle, plus an orange outsole.

BELOW: Off-White x Converse.

Givenchy (Japan only)

In 2011, fairly early on in its brand collaboration days, Converse joined forces with the Italian designer Riccardo Tisci, then at the Paris fashion house Givenchy, to produce a limited-edition shoe.

It was created for the Converse Addict series and featured a Givenchy leopard print that had been seen on the runway the previous year. Remaining true to the dark aesthetic for which Tisci is known, a cross featured on the tongue and black rubber spikes ran down the heel seam. The problem was that this was only available in Japan, and for a limited time, which meant fans elsewhere needed to get trawling online or go without.

Ambush

Yoon Ahn, of the jewellery-meets-streetwear brand Ambush, started to explore new territory at the end of 2018 when she decided she wanted to add footwear to her collection. She had a certain kind of boot in mind, which was on her mood board, and as luck would have it, Nike (who by now owned Converse) got in touch and invited her to visit the Converse HQ in Boston. Ahn took with her the picture of the military-inspired boots she had been thinking about and was told by the Converse design team that this was something they used to produce. It was a moment of serendipity.

LEFT: Ambush x Converse.

Ahn took the Chuck Taylor and the Pro Leather styles as her starting point and added layers of rubber to make them chunky and robust. 'In iterations of black and white, the sneakers have a futuristic feel that is tempered with a winking dose of humor,' wrote *American Vogue*'s Liam Hess about the design. Ahn noted that she was keen to make sure that whatever she did to the shoes, they remained recognizable: 'I try to keep the heritage side of those pieces, but also think, "What can we bring in 2019?"'

A further collaboration came the following year, featuring the Chuck Taylor All Star Duck Boot and the Chuck 70. The wading boot riffed on the Lugged raised sole, and seemed to pay homage to Converse's origins as a rubber shoe company over a century ago. The upper of the latter was crafted in wild shearling to create a fuzzy, almost toy-like shoe – especially as it came in blue and called to mind a Jim Henson puppet, in the best possible way.

Kim Jones

British streetwear designer Kim Jones – who has worked with numerous high-profile brands and enjoyed roles as both the creative director of Fendi womenswear and the creative director of Dior Homme – debuted a collection with Converse in 2021. As well as updating the Chuck 70, Jones worked

RIGHT: Ambush x Converse Chuck Taylor All Star Duck Boot.

on a range of apparel, including T-shirts, sweatshirts, cargo pants and a parka.

'I looked at the Japanese designers readapting American sportswear – recreating that fifties and sixties look,' explained Jones in a press release. 'Obviously, Converse was the key shoe within all that stuff. Now, I'm just putting it all together in a different way.' He added that his approach to designing the shoe had been straightforward, with the idea being that he wanted to encase it and protect it. Visually, this meant something chunkier with a techy and industrial feel - an undulating rubber side wall.

I looked at the Japanese designers readapting American sportswear – recreating that fifties and sixties look. Obviously, Converse was the key shoe within all that stuff.

With this collab having the definite feel of an event, the *London Evening Standard* instructed its readers: 'Sneakerheads, here's one for your diaries.' Jones had already been working with Nike since 2016 on limited-edition runs of its cult sneakers. The result for Converse, the paper went on, was a 'contemporary take on the traditional silhouette with a play on shape and texture that puts functionality and ease in styling at the forefront.'

The Simpsons

To celebrate 25 years of *The Simpsons* in Germany (the popular cartoon has aired in the US since 1989 and the UK since 1990), in 2014 Converse introduced the Chuck Taylor All Stars x The Simpsons. There were four designs, each featuring different graphics of the much-loved characters: two Chuck Taylor All Star Ox shoes featured prints of Maggie and Lisa on a pink version and Bart on a black one, while the high tops came complete with either a family portrait or Bart skating, which seemed like an appropriate full-circle moment.

Carhartt

High-fashion cross-collaborations, such as Fendace (Fendi x Versace) in 2022 or Gucci's 'hacking' of Balenciaga in 2021, have only recently become a thing in fashion. But it has long been typical for a high-street brand to combine forces with a designer so that each benefit from what the other lacks.

Converse has been doing this for a while, teaming up with brands in its wheelhouse or adjacent to it, such as Carhartt, which seems like a cool, friendly move (similar to the Alexis Sablone launch, where the skater designed a limited-edition pack featuring a Converse AS-1 Pro and a Nike SB Dunk Low, effectively a Converse x Nike collaboration).

Debuting in 2017, Converse CONS x Carhartt WIP has enabled the best of function, performance

and design from both brands. The One Star and Fastbreak Pro have been among the models reworked and upgraded. Then, in 2024 came an homage to 90s skate shoes via enhanced versions of the One Star Academy Pro and the Chuck Taylor All Star Pro. Details included lateral triple stitching, co-branded logos and CX foam sockliners, and the accompanying campaign featured riders from the Carhartt WIP skate team.

Feng Chen Wang

Feng Chen Wang, the eponymous menswear brand from the Chinese-born, London-based designer, partnered with Converse for several years now, having started to grow a steady relationship with the brand back in 2018.

In an interview with fashion and lifestyle platform Hypebeast in January 2024, Wang said, 'Over the years, Converse has been incredibly supportive. From our first collaboration to our most recent one, the team has been extremely trusting and allowed me to design without limitations,' adding 'there isn't anything that cannot be done.'

A 2024 offering saw the 2-in-1 Chuck 70 silhouette make a return, having already been explored by Wang earlier in the year with a distressed design.

LEFT: Feng Chen Wang x Converse.

The designer is known for her deconstructed take on fashion, and this latest iteration of the Chuck 70 features a clean-cut look. Described as 'conceptual', the 2-in-1 shoe was inspired by Wang's Spring/ Summer 2019 collection, where she created new silhouettes by joining two halves of separate existing garments. The new shoes are noted as having a more concise look and feature Feng Chen Wang-imprinted Velcro straps over the laces.

Undercover

Undercover's Jun Takahashi is another designer who's no stranger to Converse. An initial team-up between Converse and the cult Japanese brand in 2018 resulted in colourful Chuck 70s with contrasting

BELOW: Undercover x Converse, 2019.

toecaps inscribed with the words 'order' and 'disorder'. This was followed with a release in 2019 that explored the Chuck 70s style in black and off-white. Here, standard laces were switched out in favour of a zipper down the front, with the lace eyelets dotted up alongside it, encapsulating Undercover's post-punk aesthetic. The laces were threaded up through the eyelets, not across the zipper, and the toecaps bore the words 'the new warriors' beneath a metal ring.

Margaret Howell

In 2015, Margaret Howell, the much-revered British designer known for her simple lines and unfussy sense of nostalgia, teamed up with Converse again after collaborating on a double-pack of its Chuck Taylor All Stars a few years previously. The understated sneakers were reissued for the summer; the upper detailing came in washed cream or black cotton, with a herringbone strip along the heel column and a single black line along the midsole.

In 2023, Howell worked with Converse on new iterations of the All Star Earl silhouette, with colourways in Anthracite and Pale Green, and featuring a rubber toecap and sole unit.

Telfar

Expanding its reach even further, in 2019 Converse debuted a collaboration during New York Fashion Week with Telfar, the brand founded by Telfar

Clemens in 2004. The Spring/Summer 2020 collection included apparel and footwear, which *Teen Vogue* described as 'Converse's basketball heritage and silhouettes, reimagined in conjunction with Telfar's core design principles of inclusivity, innovation and non-gender specificity.'

The iconic star motif featured alongside Telfar branding and a disruptive take on the Pro Leather shoe, imagined this time as a slip-on silhouette. Meanwhile, the ERX, a basketball style of the 1980s, was reworked into a sandal, and canvas – the signature fabric of Converse – was used for T-shirts. Further collaborations have included a co-branded duffel bag, which sold out in 2021, plus Pro Leather Mary Janes and rubber slides.

ABOVE: Maison Margiela x Converse.

Telfar's core design principles of inclusivity, innovation and non-gender specificity.

LEFT: Maison Margiela x Converse.

Maison Margiela

In fashion circles, the name Maison Margiela is uttered with awe and respect. The fashion house, founded by secretive Belgian designer Martin Margiela, is known for its deconstructionist aesthetic. In 2013, the house customized Converse Chuck Taylor All Star Highs and Jack Purcells by painting them white – reportedly by hand. The idea was that the more they were worn, the more the paint cracked to reveal the original blue, red or yellow canvas beneath, making each pair entirely unique. There was also a follow-up collection in leather, which was thought to encourage more efficient cracking.

Moncler and Fragment Design

In 2020, the luxury brand Moncler, Fragment Design (the brainchild of Japanese multidisciplinary artist and designer Hiroshi Fujiwara) and Converse debuted a tri-collaboration, which Hypebeast described as being 'Two crisp, tuxedo-esque styles loaded with special branding.' The low-cut styles certainly had a slick appearance, more in line with a smart shoe. Single-coloured canvas uppers featured contrast stitching, while heel tabs included motifs from Moncler and Fragment. It was heralded as a collaboration you didn't want to miss out on – but increasingly, that has become the way with Converse. Each time, they get better and better,

RIGHT: Isabel Marant x Converse.

tapping into the zeitgeist to create enormously collectible sneakers.

Isabel Marant

It was during fashion month for the Spring/Summer 2025 season that Isabel Marant, the quintessential French designer, unveiled her collaboration with Converse. This was entirely appropriate, given that Marant has notoriously dabbled with wedge sneakers in the past and Converse has increasingly done so recently, with various avant-garde and fashion platform designs.

I always loved the Chuck Taylor All Star, it was one of the first sneakers I wore as a kid. It's such an iconic sneaker that has remained relevant for years.

Speaking to *British Vogue* in 2024, Marant explained, 'I always loved the Chuck Taylor All Star, it was one of the first sneakers I wore as a kid. It's such an iconic sneaker that has remained relevant for years. I really appreciate that type of achievement in a garment, because it's super rare.' For her, the shoe is up there with Levi's 501s: 'I mean, you look on the street and everyone's in a pair of jeans and sneakers!'

Her stamp on Converse came via a reworking of the noughties' wedge sneaker she made famous.

The new version featured the Chuck 70 silhouette as well as her vibrant prints, tufted fabrics and colourful edging and laces. The collection included a Chuck 70 high-top and low-top sneaker, a Chuck 70 with internal wedge and a Chuck 70 Ox.

Irak NYC

A woman in a trench coat crosses the road and heads into a shopping mall. She exits the building and then graffities the side of a truck. It's perennial cool girl Chloë Sevigny in a short film to mark the Autumn 2024 release of the Converse x Irak NYC One Star Pro sneaker. Irak NYC is the street brand that grew out of an infamous graffiti crew established in downtown New York in the nineties. The actress, in something of an undercover role here, is also wearing the limited-edition Andover jacket from the same collection. The tagline is, 'You never know who is down with Irak NYC'. It's hard to see how collabs can get much cooler than this.

The only question remaining is: who will be next? For Converse, no brand or talent is off limits, which makes the future look all the more exciting.

Epilogue

Converse, from humble beginnings and with various stops and starts, has become one of the most admired and coolest of the sneaker brands – partly because it follows its own rules. Its recipe is a mix of being nimble and respectful and never really straying from one classic design; it has remained true to its early roots, content to let others evolve and run amok.

Converse is a brand whose message is fundamentally about finding and celebrating the best in everyone, be that the rebellious nature of the human spirit, embracing the underdog, the thrill of competition, or the excitement of the new. So, let's allow the brand to have the final words, from their own website: 'We don't know where you'll go, but we know you'll take Converse to the future with you.'

RIGHT: Jon Cryer in *Pretty in Pink* (1986).

Index

Picture Credits

Alamy Stock Photo
adsR 31, 47, 80b, 80tl, 81, 82bl, 82br, 82tl; Allstar Picture Library Ltd 27, 113, 116; Associated Press 18, 50; A. Astes 131; Aviation History Collection 11; Guy Bell 70; Grzegorz Czapski 82tr, 83; Everett Collection Inc 22, 35, 114, 117; Patti McConville 36, 65, 80tr; MediaPunch Inc 105; Photo 12: 26; PictureLux/The Hollywood Archive 118; Retro AdArchives 33, 39; Sipa US 95, 125; Adam Stoltman 64t, 64b; TeamDAF 6; Roman Tiraspolsky 56; Tsuni/USA 107.

Getty Images
Brian Ach 67; Vanni Bassetti 126; Dave Benett 76; Edward Berthelot 127, 136, 139; Bettmann 12; Jean Chung 143; Mike Coppola 57; David Dee Delgado 53; James Devaney 63; Scott Dudelson 44; Scott Gries 111; Thearon W. Henderson 59; Herrmann

Agenturfotografie/Alamy Stock Photo 102-03; Gilbert lundt 28; Jeff Kravitz 46; Stephen Lovekin 108; Kevin Mazur 74; Patrick McMullan 49; MEGA 87; Mirrorpix 73; Jeremy Moeller 54, 128; Marc Piasecki 153; Kirstin Sinclair 40, 140, 150; Matthew Sperzel 148; Bryan Steffy 24; Streetstyleshooters 132; Justin Sullivan 93; WWD 151.

Shutterstock
5th Year Prods/Avalon Tv/Gigapix/Mail Order Comedy/Kobal 121; Cannon/Kobal 91; Dutch Oven/Kobal 119; emka74: 17; HBO/Kobal 120; Ivybby 43; Paramount/Kobal 157; John Salangsang 96; Shutterstock 146; Jim Smeal/BEI 99; Startraks Photo 100; Warner Bros/Kobal 115; yar-andy 135.

Wikicommons
16

First published in Great Britain in 2025 by
Laurence King
An imprint of Quercus Editions Ltd
Carmelite House
50 Victoria Embankment
London EC4Y 0DZ
An Hachette UK company

The authorised representative in the EEA is
Hachette Ireland, 8 Castlecourt Centre,
Castleknock Road, Castleknock, Dublin 15,
D15 YF6A, Ireland (email: info@hbgi.ie)

A CIP catalogue record for this book is available from the British Library

HB ISBN 9781529444407
Ebook ISBN 9781529444414

10 9 8 7 6 5 4 3 2 1

Cover design and art direction: Luke Bird
Design: Ginny Zeal
Project manager: Victoria Lympus
Printed and bound in Italy by L.E.G.O. S.p.A.

Papers used by Quercus are from well-managed forests and other responsible sources.